Original title:
The Meaning of Life (and Other Myths)

Copyright © 2025 Creative Arts Management OÜ
All rights reserved.

Author: Dante Kingsley
ISBN HARDBACK: 978-1-80566-092-7
ISBN PAPERBACK: 978-1-80566-387-4

The Sculptor of Our Own Reality

We chisel our dreams with a spoon,
While the universe laughs at our tune.
In a world made of clay, we play,
Creating a mess at the end of the day.

With each wacky mold that we craft,
We find wisdom in folly and daft.
The statue of life, bizarre and bright,
Is truly a masterpiece of pure delight.

Destinies Intertwined

Two threads in a knot like a laugh,
We fumble our way through this paragraph.
With every twist, a painting unfolds,
Of clumsy moments and stories told.

Our paths bump and giggle, so unrefined,
Life's a sitcom, our fate intertwined.
In the chaos of plans, we sit and we smile,
Who needs a map when we can run wild?

In Search of the Lost Narrative

We wander through pages, where's the plot?
Searching for meaning, but we find a dot.
With every chapter, we burst into song,
Like a jester who knows he doesn't belong.

Characters tumble, plotlines collide,
In this wild tale, we all take a ride.
With laughter our compass, we roam far and wide,
In the book of our lives, we're the stars of the stride.

Stars that Fell from Graces

Once shining bright, now on the ground,
These celestial jokers make quite the sound.
With giggles and winks, they dance through the night,
Turning mishaps to magic, a hilarious sight.

They twinkle with mischief, a cosmic delight,
In the comedy show of existence, so bright.
With each crash and tumble, we share in the glee,
For life is a circus, and we hold the key.

The Palette of Life's Contradictions

In a world where socks go solo,
We wonder if the cat's a hero.
Chasing dreams in a paper boat,
While they float off, we just gloat.

A slice of pizza for the soul,
Dancing dough on a silver roll.
With toppings that question fate,
Sprinkles of joy on a plate.

Searching for Sunlight in Shadows

Tickle the clouds, they laugh aloud,
Where sunbeams play in a misty shroud.
Finding joy in a puddle's glare,
Reflecting dreams that float in air.

With umbrellas made of jellybeans,
We sip on life's silly cuisines.
In every shadow, a quirk is found,
Dancing like ducks on the ground.

Weaving Tales in a World of Paradoxes

A snail that ran a marathon,
Wears its shell like a tuxedo gone.
Sideways glances at elephants fly,
As kangaroos bounce and waves sigh.

Spinning yarns of improbable fate,
With butterflies that argue and debate.
In the tapestry, laughter is sewn,
Knitting jokes into seeds we've grown.

The Dance of Creation and Destruction

With each balloon that we let go,
A story bursts, a tide of flow.
Of brick and candy, we build our dreams,
Toppling towers made of moonbeams.

In every giggle, chaos swirls,
As kittens duet, and yarn unfurls.
In this waltz of joy and strife,
We find the rhythm of quirky life.

Dances Upon the Edge of Existence

Waltzing with fate, what a sight,
Tripping on dreams, oh what a fright!
We shimmy through choices, so absurd,
Living with joy, but life's a blur.

A jig with the cosmos, laughter galore,
Each step we take opens a door.
Falling like leaves, we giggle and spin,
Who knew the chaos could be such a win!

Twisting through questions, seeking a sign,
We come as we are, all tangled in twine.
Leaving our worries far behind,
Trusting the dance will help us unwind.

So here we are, just fools in a show,
Chasing the echoes, letting it flow.
Life's nothing but a quirky jest,
Strut on, dear friend, and forget the rest!

The Heart's Unfolding Story

In the garden of feelings, we grow,
Poking at petals, pushing the flow.
Love is a riddle wrapped in a purr,
Each turn brings laughter, life's little blur.

Tales told by stars, oh what a game,
We scribble our dreams, never the same.
With wild little giggles, our secrets unfold,
Life's like a tale that never gets old.

Chasing the whispers of what could be,
Our hearts beat a rhythm, oh can't you see?
Falling for quirks, we make quite a fuss,
Together we laugh, just the two of us.

So scribble your stories, wild and free,
Dance to the nonsense, let it all be.
For in every heartbeat, a punchline may hide,
Life's just a giggle on this cosmic ride!

Reverberations of a Cosmic Whisper

In the silence of night, a chuckle so sly,
Stars wink in mischief, oh my, oh my!
They whisper the secrets of ages gone by,
Life's punchline, it seems, just sails through the sky.

Nebulas giggle as comets rush past,
Time's a comedian, moves ever so fast.
While planets may wobble, we sway to the beat,
Twirling in echoes, let's all take a seat.

With each twinkle, a joke shared in space,
The universe grins, it's a whimsical place.
So ponder your fate, take a leap if you dare,
Laughter's the language we all have to share.

For in cosmic whispers, truths shine like gold,
In each tiny moment, life's mysteries unfold.
Let's laugh with the stars, catch the quirky delight,
For we're but a giggle in this wonderful night!

Serendipity's Hand in Every Step

Stumbling through life, we trip and we dance,
Each twist, every turn, is a remarkable chance.
Finding odd treasures in mud and in gloom,
Life's surprises pop up, like flowers in bloom.

A sudden wrong turn leads us to cheer,
Where strangers become friends, and laughter is near.
The universe winks, oh what a delight,
In chaos, we find the best kind of light.

Every misstep's a treasure in disguise,
Painting our paths with the boldest of ties.
So grab onto serendipity's hand,
Its silly adventures make life oh so grand.

We'll dance with the fates, fully aware,
That joy finds a way, in the most foolish air.
With chuckles and giggles, let's take every leap,
For in every blunder, memories we'll keep!

Light's Reflection in Dark Waters

Bubbles rise, stories swim,
A fish in a tux, where's the whim?
Reflections dance on the muddy glint,
As we ponder what gives life a hint.

Splashing thoughts like a leaky hose,
What's under the surface? Who really knows!
The pond's gossip travels far and wide,
As frogs throw shade, it's quite the ride.

With plucky ducks doing a waddle show,
And sunbeams gossiping, stealing the glow,
Chasing our tails, we're quite the sight,
In this water ballet, we feel so light.

The Veins of the Earth Speak

Rivers gurgle secrets long forgot,
While mountains grumble, and they're not caught.
Roots intertwine like gossipy friends,
Sharing kernels of truth when daylight ends.

The earth chuckles with each quake and shake,
Pretending to nap, it's all a mistake.
The trees wave hello with leafy applause,
As squirrels debate with philosophical pause.

In the wind's whispers and the soil's sigh,
A nutty kind of wisdom floats by.
From ants in a line to the clouds on high,
Life's just a comedy—oh me, oh my!

The Enigma of Our Shared Breath

Inhale, exhale, what's this dance?
A synchronized gasping, quite the romance.
Tickling the air, we puff and we wheeze,
Like balloons at a party, we giggle with ease.

Every sneeze tells tales of last night's feast,
From pizza to garlic, the mystery increased.
Together we laugh, share space and air,
In this wacky ballet, we're a whimsical pair.

Laughter bubbles up, like soda so sweet,
A chorus of joy in every heartbeat.
Hold your breath, then let it out grand,
Life's just a pantomime, quite unplanned!

Harmonies of Existence's Chord

The universe strums on a cosmic guitar,
With notes that giggle, carried from afar.
Stars in concert, each one a clown,
Juggling planets in this stellar town.

Harmony whispers, with a chuckle or two,
As comets skate by, making quite the view.
Plucking the strings of our curious fate,
In this wild jam session, we patiently wait.

So dance with the cosmos, don't miss the beat,
Every twirl and spin is a funny treat.
Laughter and stardust, woven in time,
In this grand symphony, all is sublime.

Beyond the Horizon of Understanding

In a world where logic trips,
And reason does a silly dance,
We ponder why we take those sips,
Of tea while wearing underpants.

The cat on the roof plays chess,
With a squirrel that shouts, "Checkmate!"
Life's riddles come with jest and stress,
As we debate our dinner fate.

Why do socks wear mismatched pride?
And where do lost keys like to roam?
In this cosmic ride, let's confide,
The best seat is the one called home.

So grab a snack and take a seat,
Laugh at the whimsy in the air,
For in this game, it's all quite sweet,
To cherish nonsense everywhere.

The Parable of Every Breath

Every breath's a tickle fight,
With whispers that chase clouds away,
We stumble through the day and night,
As time plays silly games at play.

A snail debates the speed of light,
While wearing shades and sipping wine,
It claims a race is quite the sight,
But starts to snooze by half past nine.

Lemons laugh as they roll down hills,
While oranges hold a fruit parade,
And every fumble, every thrill,
Is proof that life is homemade.

So take that leap, and dance astray,
With every wrong turn, find the art,
In a world that's just here to play,
With smiles that tickle every heart.

Uncharted Realms of Consciousness

In dreams where unicorns do prance,
And broccoli wears tiny hats,
We twirl and spin in wild dance,
With ice cream cones and silly chats.

A penguin plays the piano keys,
While whales serenade the stars,
The world's a giddy, giggly breeze,
With adventure tossed in candy jars.

We question logic, poke the void,
With rubber ducks to lead the way,
In this strange realm, we're all annoyed,
By socks that vanish every day.

So grab the stars and paint them red,
With laughter echoing through the halls,
For in this space where dreams are bred,
Silly tales are the winning calls.

Kaleidoscope of Whimsical Wonder

In the land where wishes giggle,
And paradoxes skip and twirl,
The clouds, they dance, and then they wiggle,
Sprinkling sparkles in a whirl.

A llama wears a bowtie, bold,
While trees recite their own sweet verse,
Each tale a new delight to hold,
In colors bright, the world's a curse.

With jellybeans that sing at night,
And fish that flaunt their sparkling scales,
We spin in joy, with pure delight,
As life unveils its quirky trails.

So let us dive in laughter's grace,
In this kaleidoscope we spin,
For under every quirky face,
Lies the magic where fun begins.

Cosmic Riddles Unraveled

Stars align in quirky ways,
Why does cheese make us sing?
Galaxies spin with silly grace,
Is it all just a cosmic fling?

Planets dance with goofy glee,
Black holes spit out lost socks,
Meteor showers sprinkle tea,
Gravity's just a prankster's box!

Laughter echoes through the void,
Asteroids wear mismatched shoes,
Comets come with jokes deployed,
In space, there's nothing to lose!

Unsung Songs of the Heartbeat

Each thump sings a silly tune,
As hearts waltz in prancing light,
Valentine's cards fly to the moon,
Chocolate wishes take their flight!

Tickle the strings of fate's guitar,
With rhythms that make us grin,
An off-key love can travel far,
Silly serenades in the din!

Heartbeat's mantra, loud and clear,
"Date a pizza, it won't flee!"
In the dance of bliss and cheer,
Pizza's crust is company!

Reflections in a Pool of Time

Ripples laugh at our bright faces,
Time tips its hat with a wink,
Mirrors show our silliest races,
Who knew clocks could have a drink?

Watches whisper, "Don't you fret,"
Tick-tock's really just a game,
Seconds giggle, "Who's your pet?"
The nonsense gets a wild fame!

With every splash, the past does chuckle,
Moments tickle our silly bones,
Dive into time's fun little shuffle,
Life's just a circle of trombones!

The Chronicles of Fleeting Moments

Gather 'round for tales of yore,
When squirrels ran for office, you see,
Each giggle leaves us wanting more,
In a world shaped like a funny bee!

Pancakes flipping, the grandest feast,
Where syrup dances on the side,
Every bite's a laughter beast,
Oh, the joy we cannot hide!

Fleeting moments, like comic strips,
Crayon doodles drawn at noon,
Life's a show with plenty of quips,
And every laugh's a silly boon!

Forks in the Path of Destiny

When paths diverge like spaghetti strands,
We toss a coin and hope it lands.
Each choice we make is quite absurd,
Like choosing 'yes' for every word.

The signs we see don't seem quite real,
A squirrel's advice or a pizza meal.
A fork in the road, do you take the chance?
Or dance with a chicken in a silly dance?

A road sign points to nowhere fast,
In dreams of future, we're unsurpassed.
Each turn we take, a riddle and rhyme,
Just getting lost… We'll blame it on time.

Beneath the Surface of the Mundane

Coffee spills and socks misplaced,
In daily grind, we're all well-paced.
A joyless chore, we all know this?
But wait… is that a rogue goldfish?

The dishes pile like mountain peaks,
While life's true treasures hide in creeks.
Behind each nap is a secret stolen,
Like finding joy in math, once scowlin'.

Beneath the curtains, chaos reigns,
But laughter often breaks the chains.
A circus act, oh what a fluke,
In life's dull drudgery, find the spook!

An Odyssey of Unanswered Queries

Why is a raven like a writing desk?
Questions spin, we're left to jest.
With every 'why,' we twist and shout,
Like kids at play, there's no real doubt.

Perhaps the sun is just shy and fair,
Or rainclouds are in a grumpy affair.
Each pondered thought a frantic chase,
In riddles lost, we find our place.

Is existence merely cats with hats?
Or are we all just talking gnats?
Inquiries swirl, like leaves on a breeze,
Hoopla and answers are meant to tease.

Life's Paradox and Poetry

A jester quips, 'What's life's great scheme?'
A riddle wrapped in a whimsical dream.
We laugh at the irony, trip on our feet,
As wisdom dances to a silly beat.

The chicken crossed, but what's it mean?
To catch a bus or just to preen?
Life's great paradox, it spins and spins,
Like a hamster wheel where no one wins.

With verses that twist like a corkscrew's fate,
Find joy in the absurd, it's never too late.
In poetry's grasp, the truth might view,
That life's a puzzle, a laugh or two!

When Questions Dance in Silence

Why did the chicken cross the street?
To find answers, not just a treat!
With every step, a riddle's thrill,
While pondering if time stands still.

Dancing questions in the air,
Curbside gossip, who would care?
The why, the how, the what to do,
All jumbled in a cosmic stew.

Each thought a twirl, each guess a spin,
Like a game where nobody wins.
In the silence of a conundrum,
Life's a joke—just ask the drum!

So laugh a little, when lost and spun,
Confusion's fun; we've just begun!
With question marks that pirouette,
We find the fun in not knowing yet.

The Secret Language of the Soul

Whispers travel on the breeze,
What is the soul saying, if you please?
Is it French, or maybe a dance?
Complete with sparkles, a little romance.

Does it giggle, or maybe sigh?
Contemplating reasons to fly high.
Its voice can rhyme, or sometimes mess,
Like cats speaking through a knitted vest.

In the chambers of the heart,
Every beat is a work of art.
A waltz of hope, a shuffle of fears,
It speaks in riddles, and sometimes sneers.

So listen closely to its tune,
It might reveal a laugh or a swoon.
The secret tongue is a funny chap,
With puns and laughter, it has a map.

A Canvas of Forgotten Dreams

On a canvas splashed with bright hues,
Lie dreams that flopped like old shoes.
A rainbow of hope gone slightly bad,
Painted by wishes, some quirky, some sad.

The artist forgot the brush one day,
Stuck with crayons, hip hip hooray!
Each line a journey, a wild slip,
An adventure that's more of a trip.

The gallery filled with things we tossed,
All the chances that we thought we lost.
Each stroke a chuckle, each color a guffaw,
Life's folly painted with a messy jaw.

So grab a brush, don't take it too serious,
Life's a joke, it's quite delirious.
With dreams that giggle and colors that gleam,
We paint our path with a humorous theme.

Between the Dawn and Dusk

In that space where day meets night,
What's wrong seems a little right.
The sun does a goofy little dance,
As stars start winking in their cosmic pants.

Is it breakfast, or maybe a dream?
Is that moon a slice of whipped cream?
As twilight swirls in quirky spins,
Life's greatest riddle really begins.

Chasing shadows, chasing light,
What's the answer? Perhaps it's bright!
In every giggle and slip of fate,
We find the fun in a silly debate.

So let's toast to the twilight's song,
It's where we really all belong.
Between the dawn and the dusk's embrace,
We laugh aloud in this whimsical place.

Underneath the Veil of Normalcy

Life is just a silly dance,
With two left feet, we take our chance.
Searching for the meaning in a pizza slice,
With toppings of chaos, and a hint of spice.

We wear our masks like a game of charades,
Pretending to know how adulthood parades.
In coffee shops, we ponder the deep,
While sharing our secrets, we'd rather not keep.

Recurring Dreams of Otherworldly Journeys

I take a rocket made of cheese,
To chase my fears with utmost ease.
A cat in glasses reads my fate,
Sipping tea at a cosmic gate.

With unicorns that take me higher,
In starry skies, my soul's desire.
Yet I wake up to laundry stacks,
Searching for my missing socks and snacks.

The Heart's Blueprint of Belonging

In a world of pets and weird pet names,
Searching for love in all the wrong games.
I text a burger, is it too late?
Did it leave me for fries on a dinner date?

Friendship's a puzzle, each piece a surprise,
With mismatched corners and skewed alibis.
Together we laugh at our awkward fate,
In this wild journey, we navigate.

Journeying through the Echo Chamber of Time

Time's a cheeky player in a joker's hat,
It spins us 'round with a subtle spat.
I slip on time like a class clown,
Wearing a tiara, on my head upside down.

Ticking clocks are just a trick,
Making us dance to a silly click.
So let's groove through the years with grace,
For in this circus, we all find our place.

The Undercurrents of Our Journey

We sail through puddles, not the sea,
With rubber ducks a company.
Maps are scribbles, clues are rare,
But snacks will always take us there.

The compass spins, it makes no sense,
Yet laughter is our true defense.
We trip on life's peculiar dance,
And somehow always find romance.

Our sails are made of cereal boxes,
As we dodge life's wobbly foxes.
We trade our shoes for silly dreams,
In this circus, nothing's as it seems.

So let's embrace the unknown tide,
With wobbly steps, let's take a ride.
Through giggles, hiccups we will glide,
In this journey, joy's our guide.

A Symphony of Silent Questions

Why do socks vanish in the wash?
Maybe they dance at a global posh.
Is toast always buttered on one side?
Or do they flip, in secret, they hide?

The cats keep secrets, always sly,
Do they know why we even try?
Each riddle tickles, and we can't find
The reason behind the curious mind.

We search for truths in funny shapes,
While discovering odd, goofy escapes.
What are keys without the locks?
Just shiny bits for silly talks!

Sometimes the answers just don't come,
Perhaps that's why we hum or drum.
Questions float like bubbles, bright,
Pop! They burst into pure delight.

Chasing Shadows in the Sunlight

We run from shadows, chase the light,
Playing tag till the day turns night.
With giggles echoing through the park,
We dance with shadows, oh, what a lark!

Sunscreen slathered, hats too wide,
In the heat, our laughter can't hide.
We trip over grass, like clumsy fools,
Imagining we're in ancient schools.

The grass whispers secrets, we must hear,
As ants hold tiny meetings near.
Life's a circus, and we're the clowns,
In floppy shoes and silly crowns.

So twist and twirl and spin around,
Each sunny day's a joyful sound.
In the chase, we find delight,
In shadows that vanish with the night.

Fables of Forgotten Paths

Once upon a time, paths were lost,
Adventurers tumbled, but never tossed.
With missteps taken and pies in the face,
They danced through mazes at a frantic pace.

A frog in a hat gave wise advice,
"Embrace the muck, it's rather nice!"
So off they went, without a clue,
Trading straight lines for zig-zagging too.

They found a fork, and what a tease,
One path was covered in gooey cheese.
The other, a river of brimming pies,
They chose donuts, to everyone's surprise!

The tales they told, with laughter and cheer,
Of paths that twisted, yet brought them here.
In every fable, a wink and a grin,
For joy, my friend, is how we win!

Threads Woven in the Tapestry of Being

In a world of tangled strings,
We stitch our silly schemes.
Patterns fade and colors clash,
Yet we dance in vivid dreams.

With every knot, a tale unfolds,
Of socks lost and keys misplaced.
Life's a quilt of jokes retold,
As we dash, we stumble, and race.

Each thread a laugh, each loop a grin,
A jumble of our wandering ways.
Together we weave a raucous spin,
On the chaos of our days.

So grab a needle, join the fare,
Embrace the fabric, wear it proud.
For in this craft, our joys we share,
And poke fun at the wild crowd.

The Quest for Purpose

With a map drawn on a napkin now,
I set off on my grand crusade.
To find a purpose, make a vow,
Or settle for coleslaw and lemonade.

I ask the stars, they twinkle bright,
But all they say is 'Look around!'
A squirrel darted, gave me a fright,
And suddenly, I felt quite profound.

Perhaps my quest's to eat some pie,
Or sip a soda on a spree.
With laughter echoing in the sky,
I find a jest in every plea.

So let's all roam, let's dance in jest,
For meaning's found where fun is sought.
In simple smiles, we are truly blessed,
Life's mysteries wrapped in a thought.

Shadows of a Dreamer's Heart

In shadows where the dreamers play,
They scribble stars on scraps of night.
With whimsy bright, they find a way,
To giggle at the little fright.

A lost sock here, a toy that's broke,
They weave a tale of wild delight.
In dreams, the mundane becomes a joke,
And laughter shines through every blight.

They chase the clouds with coffee cups,
And skateboard on the edge of light.
In the absurdity, joy erupts,
A silly wink, a playful bite.

So let them dance in shadows deep,
For in their laughter, truth will start.
In every chuckle, secrets creep,
The mysteries lie in a dreamer's heart.

Chasing Illusions and Truths

I raced a mirage down the street,
With pockets full of hopes and clowns.
Chasing illusions, quite the feat,
Until I tripped over my own frowns.

The truths I sought were hidden well,
In fortune cookies, stale and cracked.
Each bite a riddle, a wish to quell,
Yet left me giggling, quite whacked.

With butterflies in my cereal bowl,
I mix laughter with my dreams.
In every stumble, I find my role,
More joyful than it sometimes seems.

So let's keep chasing, hand in hand,
These cartoon truths that come and go.
For life's a jest in cartoon land,
Where we embrace the silly flow.

Notes from the Silent Universe

In a void of endless chatter,
Stars giggle, planets sneak.
Black holes munch on cosmic matter,
While comets play hide and seek.

Galaxies twirl in a ballet,
Asteroids dodge like playful mice.
Space dust combines in a café,
Where time serves espresso, not rice.

A nebula wearing a hat,
Sips stardust with a graceful pout.
Planets ponder where they're at,
Finding laughs in cosmic doubt.

So, laugh with the void, my friend,
The universe knows how to jest.
In the silence, messages send,
Life's a game, and we're all guests.

Labyrinths of Hope and Despair

In a maze where hopes collide,
Joy dances with despair.
Lost socks are the tour guides,
As mismatched paths go nowhere.

Twists and turns, a funny sight,
Each corner holds a riddle.
A chicken crossed with all its might,
Just to play a cosmic fiddle.

Some find luck in a dead end,
Others trip on dreams that fly.
Laughter echoes, hearts can mend,
As we ponder, 'Oh, why?'

We weave through threads of fate,
Jokes stitched in every seam.
Through each laugh, life we create,
Turning struggle into a dream.

Flickering Flames of Our Essence

In a candlelit corner we sit,
Flames flicker, stories unfold.
Laughter weaves through every bit,
As sparks of joy dance bold.

Wicks of dreams never too bright,
Melt with every secret shared.
We glow in the still of night,
While the weirdest thoughts are aired.

Ghosts of hopes jump in a jig,
Shadowed doubts twist around.
If life's a riddle, let's do a gig,
As the silliness knows no bound.

With warmth in our hearts, we say,
Let the flames flicker and sway.
For each snicker clears the way,
To find joy in every day.

The Weight of a Single Breath

Inhale deeply, what a chore,
Each breath carries a thousand tales.
Exhale laughter, more and more,
While life plays with cosmic scales.

A sneeze could alter time and space,
As giggles drift through the air.
Each wheeze a dance, a wild race,
Creating stories everywhere.

Breathe out dreams like bubbles float,
Watch them pop with silly grace.
Each moment's a whimsical note,
Life's rhythm finds its own pace.

So, with every breath, let's toast,
To the weight of each funny thought.
For in life's ever-shifting coast,
Joy is what we all sought.

Whirlwinds of Wonder.

In a world spun tight like a rubber band,
We chase our dreams, always underhand.
Hopping like frogs in a game of chance,
Trying to find the secret dance.

With cookies and cream in a grand parade,
Explaining life with a charming charade.
We juggle our hopes under skies of blue,
Pretending we know what we thought we knew.

With giggles and gaffes, we cross the street,
Where meaning lurks in a clown's silly feat.
Life's just a joke, served with a grin,
We laugh, we cry, and then we begin.

So grab your hat, let the laughter flow,
In a whirlwind of wonder, let's steal the show.
Here's to the chaos, the chuckles, the fun,
For in this great circus, we're all just one.

Whispers of Existence

In the hush of the night, we hear soft tones,
Like mice in a pantry, rattling bones.
Existence whispers in riddles and rhymes,
As we trip on our shoelaces, missing good times.

The cat on the roof philosophizes deep,
While we grasp at thoughts that skip like sheep.
In velvet voids where silly rules reign,
We sip from cups filled with giggles and pain.

To ponder so much, yet trip on a word,
Like flying fish in a flock of birds.
Life's on the tip of our clumsy lips,
We're dancing with thoughts in our awkward trips.

So let's toast to the whispers that tickle our ears,
With laughter and nonsense to mask all our fears.
For in every giggle, a truth we might find,
In the whispers of life, we're all intertwined.

Echoes of Fleeting Time

Tick-tock, tick-tock, the clock gives a wink,
As we question if we'll ever stop to think.
In a race with shadows, we stumble along,
Chasing our tails, singing the wrong song.

Echoes of laughter bounce off the walls,
As we visit the past in our silly calls.
Time plays the jester in a pantomime show,
Where reason takes a break and chaos steals the glow.

With calendars printed in hues of delight,
We pencil in parties and dream through the night.
Yet, in each fleeting moment, we twist and we bend,
Grasping at seconds like chasing a friend.

So here's to the echoes, the laughter, the cheer,
To moments that vanish and reappear.
In the dance of existence, we laugh as we climb,
Understanding nothing, yet racing through time.

Searching for Stars in the Ordinary

In mundane kitchens where chaos reigns,
We sift through the cabinets, ignoring the stains.
Searching for stars in a bowl full of peas,
Hoping to find cosmic truths with ease.

The laundry piles high like mountains of fluff,
Yet here in their chaos, we giggle and puff.
Each sock's a reminder of moments gone by,
Where wisdom is wrapped in a sweet apple pie.

In coffee shops buzzing, we plot and we scheme,
With dreams that unfold like a sun-kissed beam.
As mundane becomes magic in our goofy ride,
We twirl through the simple with stars as our guide.

So let's raise our mugs to the ordinary grind,
For in every mess, more than wisdom we find.
In our search for the stars, let's take time to see,
That in simple moments, we're wild and free.

Melodies of the Unwritten

In the dance of fate we trip,
With banana peels that we quip.
A slip and slide, we laugh and squeal,
Chasing dreams that are quite unreal.

With every choice, a jest we make,
Like ice cream cones that always break.
Each scoop a riddle, each swirl a twist,
In this comedy, who can resist?

We ponder deep and scratch our heads,
Like chickens dreaming in their beds.
Life's a circus, a jolly show,
Where even clowns can steal the glow.

So let the jigs and giggles flow,
In silly hats with lights that glow.
For in this mess, we find our way,
Through laughter bright, come what may.

Reflections in Still Water

Watch the pond, it winks at me,
With ripples dancing, wild and free.
I toss a stone, it makes a splash,
And ducks in bow ties start to dash.

Life's a mirror, we take a peek,
At silly faces, not so sleek.
With every glance, we laugh out loud,
A bit absurd, we're all so proud.

We chase reflections, like lost socks,
In crowds of thoughts, like ticking clocks.
So splash around, don't take offense,
In jest and joy, we find our sense.

From puddles wide to skies so blue,
Each skip a laugh, a chance to glue.
In quiet waters, we can see,
The humor lurking, wild and free.

Heartbeats of Distinction

Oh, what is this we call our beat?
A thud, a bump, a playful treat.
With every heartbeat, life's a joke,
A jester's hat on each fine bloke.

We wear our quirks like badges bright,
In silly walks, we take our flight.
With hiccuped dreams and snorted thrills,
In life's great circus, forget the drills.

Each pulse a dance, each laugh a cheer,
Who knew our hearts could hold such cheer?
From dance floors to the frozen aisle,
In every bit, let's flaunt our style.

So let your heart do somersaults,
In rollercoasters, life exalts.
For in this game of ups and downs,
A giggle reigns, no room for frowns.

Beyond the Veil of Illusion

Behind the curtain, secrets play,
A jigsaw puzzle, come what may.
We ponder deeply with our forks,
While pondering puns from cheeky storks.

In each illusion, laughter grows,
Like a fuzzy hat worn on our toes.
A trampoline made of fluffy clouds,
Where laughter leaps and joy enshrouds.

We jibe and jape, a merry crew,
With each absurdity we pursue.
So peel away that sticky tape,
Embrace the humor, no escape.

Through tangled thoughts, we find our best,
In masks of comedy, life jest.
For when we laugh, we truly see,
That life's a myth, absurd and free.

The Whisper of a Million Lives

In a café where dreams collide,
A waiter spills your fate with pride.
He serves you hope with extra foam,
And laughs as visions call you home.

A cat wearing glasses gives you a wink,
She sips her tea, ponders, then thinks.
"Why chase shadows when you can dance?"
She sways and nudges your heart's chance.

Life's a circus, full of jest,
With clowns that wear your favorite vest.
Juggling thoughts, they tumble and roll,
And giggle at the weighty goal.

So raise a glass to all that's strange,
To fortune's whim and the laughter's range.
In this riddle, wrapped in a tease,
You'll find that joy is sure to please.

Transitory Gleams of Eternity

The moth flutters, dodging the flame,
With a wink, it giggles, it's just a game.
Flinging itself at the light's warm glow,
Yelling, "Hey, at least it's a show!"

Birds flock in a haphazard swarm,
Chirping loudly, they break the norm.
"Why fly straight? Let's take a twist!"
In life's great farce, how can we resist?

A cheese that dreams of being a moon,
Splits wide with laughter, who needs a tune?
It rolls down hills, in search of a plate,
Proclaiming, "Adventures can wait!"

So laugh as stars break through the dusk,
In mismatched socks or caked with husk.
Life's a nutty, whimsical scheme,
Where even chaos can gleam with a beam.

The Embrace of Time's Emissary

Tick tock, the clock has slipped,
With a grin, its whispers tripped.
"Hurry up, we're short on fun,"
While chasing squirrels that skip and run.

Tea leaves curling in a spout,
Spin tales of fate, no room for doubt.
"Life's a puzzle, but no stress,"
Each wrong piece? Just glamour's dress!

The sun wears shades, the moon throws shade,
As they play hopscotch in the glade.
"You blink, then miss your best chance!"
Join in the waltz, let's all prance!

So check that watch, but play it cool,
The universe won't follow a rule.
In the jests of time, we're all just friends,
With giggles and quirks until the end.

When Hope Blooms in Adversity

In a garden of socks, where flowers grow,
A dandelion speaks, "Just go with the flow!"
"When life hands you lemons, make some pie!"
And butterflies nod, flapping by in the sky.

A toaster pops up, with a chuckle and cheer,
"Don't stress, my friend, I'm glad you're here!"
With burnt edges telling tales of delight,
It serves toast with jam for a cozy night.

On rainy days, umbrellas dance,
Spinning in puddles, they take a chance.
With each drip drop, a giggle is found,
As puddles reflect a world upside down.

So grab your socks and spin a tune,
Embrace the chaos, don't be a prune.
For through the squabbles and life's little quirks,
Hope blossoms brightly amidst the works.

The Quest for Significance

In a world of big questions, they say,
We search for some wisdom, come what may.
But in socks that don't match, we find our glee,
Life's peculiar riddle might just be free.

With googly eyes on potato heads,
Dancing through life, ignoring the dreads.
We ponder our purpose while munching on fries,
Yet laughter's the prize in our endless tries.

A quest with no map, we wander and roam,
Chasing ideas while forgetting our home.
But in silly moments, the truth is unveiled,
In a giggle, a snicker, where joy has prevailed.

So skip down the lane, let your doubts be light,
With a twinkle of humor, everything's bright.
And who knew that joy could be wrapped in some fluff?
Perhaps standing here laughing is more than enough.

Patterns of the Unfathomable

Life's puzzle pieces jigsaw in air,
Like trying to comb through a cat's tangled hair.
The patterns we chase, all spirals and swirls,
Yet rice in your pocket still makes your heart twirl.

The cosmic dance, a cha-cha with fate,
Twisting and spinning, oh isn't it great?
A dance with your coffee, a waltz with your cat,
Just avoid stepping on that strange creature's mat.

Questions unfold like origami birds,
Waiting to fly off while ignoring our words.
Yet with each clumsy flap, we eventually land,
With sauce on our faces and laughter at hand.

So don't fret the patterns, just embrace the chance,
To frolic through life in a clumsy old dance.
For in every misstep, a wiggle and laugh,
Are clues to the mystery, the quirky path.

Navigating the Unknown

We set sail at dawn with maps all askew,
With a compass that points to the old lady's shoe.
The horizon's a smudge, and the shores disappear,
But we giggle and shout, for we have no fear.

In the vastness we tumble, like socks in a wash,
Navigating chaos, all wild-eyed and posh.
With rubber duck captains and toast as our guide,
We'll conquer the waves on this wobbly ride.

Charting the unexplored realms of bizarre,
Searching for meaning in crumbs from afar.
Yet discovering laughter in mishaps we find,
Leads us to treasures that sparkle our mind.

So hoist up the flags, let confusion reign free,
For the jest of the journey is all we will see.
And perhaps the unknown is just a banana,
Wielding the wisdom of rare old Nirvana.

Specters of Belief

In shadows we see ghosts in funny hats,
Whispering secrets, like wise little cats.
They tell us stories beneath twisted trees,
While drinking hot cocoa and sneezing with ease.

With each tale they spin, we chuckle and grin,
At the wild waltz of absurdity within.
They rattle their chains, but we roll our eyes,
For life's just a circus in a clever disguise.

Existence, they claim, a vast cosmic joke,
With punchlines that linger as we laugh and choke.
Yet the ghosts, full of wisdom, dance in the fray,
Reminding us lightly to laugh every day.

So tip your hat to those specters who tease,
In folly and laughter, we find our degrees.
For with playful belief, oh, what can we gain?
Just a ticket to joy in life's whimsical train.

The Alchemy of Being

In a cauldron, we mix our dreams,
A pinch of giggles, or so it seems.
Stir in some chaos, add a dash of bliss,
Life's a potion, you can't resist.

We wander like wizards in silly hats,
With rubber chickens and chattering cats.
Casting our spells on the mundane grind,
Unraveling riddles, the funny kind.

Life's a carnival, spinning around,
With cotton candy, and laughter unbound.
We juggle our worries, they tumble and fall,
While juggling clowns echo our call.

In this alchemical frolic, we sip,
From goblets of joy, we dare not skip.
So raise your glasses, let's make a toast,
To the quirky magic we cherish most!

Ephemeral Alignments of Stars

Twinkling thoughts dance in the night,
Cosmic jokes come into sight.
A comet slips on a banana peel,
Oh, the humor that the heavens conceal!

Constellations giggle, shooting light,
While planets argue about who's polite.
They pull our strings like puppets in play,
Spinning our fates in the silliest way.

Gravity's a prankster, keeping us near,
While we pretend to have no fear.
Stars whisper secrets, then burst out in glee,
Isn't the cosmos just a vast comedy?

So, let's chart our quirks as we float on by,
Beneath the chuckles of a starry sky.
For every giggle that we impart,
Is a twinkle of joy in the universe's heart!

Rustling Leaves of Uncertainty

Leaves are gossiping in the breeze,
Whispering secrets with mischievous ease.
What to do next? The world may tire,
But the rustling leaves leap higher and higher.

A squirrel comments, with nuts in tow,
"Life's a game, just go with the flow!"
They laugh at the rain, and dance in the sun,
Each rustle a riddle, a pun to be spun.

And when the wind howls its dubious tune,
The leaves chuckle back, "We'll figure it soon!"
For through the uncertainty and wild surprise,
Lies the art of laughter, we claim and devise.

Our paths may be scattered like leaves in the air,
Yet we twirl like dancers, without a care.
In the grand symphony of what we perceive,
Let's spin and let laughter be what we believe!

The Infinite Play of Light and Shadow

In this theatre of flickering flames,
Shadows play tricks, they dance with names.
One moment a giant, the next a mouse,
Life's a circus—a whimsical house!

Light teases dark, in a playful debate,
Casting long shadows to exaggerate.
With a flick of the wrist, they swap and swirl,
Daring reflections in a crazy whirl.

We stumble like actors on this grand stage,
The script is a giggle, the lines all the rage.
Our thoughts are the spotlights, silly and bright,
Bathing our moments in laughter and light.

So laugh with the shadows, embrace their RSVP,
To a ball where we play, you and me.
For in this grand jest of the light and the gray,
Lies a magic that twinkles, come what may!

Whispers of Existence

In the kitchen, thoughts collide,
A recipe of joy, with a pinch of pride.
Who says we need all the answers clear?
Just add some cookies, and serve with cheer!

Cats plot schemes, they're the true kings,
Chasing shadows and fluffy little things.
Life's a laugh, a well-timed prank,
So splash some paint, don't forget to thank!

Fragments of Forever

We gather pieces like jigsaw dreams,
Finding joy in the silliest schemes.
A dance here, a wiggle there,
Life's just a joke, if we dare to share!

With mismatched socks, we strut and sway,
Claiming randomness leads the way.
When faced with fate, just give a grin,
Life's a circus, come join in!

Echoes in the Abyss

Why ponder deep, why ruminate?
Might as well ponder how to celebrate!
Throw confetti on existential dread,
And watch the universe shake its head!

Voices whisper, secrets find,
Tape your wisdom to your behind.
In shadows where curiosities play,
Dance like nobody's watching today!

Canvas of Selves

Life's a canvas, splashed with glee,
Paint with laughter, let humor be free.
Doodle the moments, sketch out a grin,
Who needs a map when you've got good chin?

Every mishap, a stroke of art,
Turn fumbles and trips into playful heart.
So let's explore our colorful strife,
As we waltz through this absurd life!

Labyrinths of Truth

In a maze of thoughts, we roam,
Chasing cheese like a hungry gnome.
What's the secret? Who truly knows?
Maybe it's where the garden grows.

Each corner turned, a question asked,
Are socks and shoes a daunting task?
If life's a riddle wrapped in a pun,
Why's it always raining when I run?

A map squiggled in crayon hue,
Leads to snacks and a dance or two.
Forget the wisdom books proclaim,
I prefer snacks over the fame.

So we wander, lost but free,
In search of snacks and revelry.
If wisdom's odd, let laughter reign,
And let the fun be our true gain!

Chasing Celestial Shadows

Stars overhead, they wink and play,
Do they know where we lost our way?
Chasing tails of comets bright,
Wondering if they bite at night.

Galaxies spinning like a DJ's turn,
We twirl and whirl, oh, what a burn!
The universe sings a cosmic tune,
But I just want to dance with the moon.

Aliens giggle in their shiny ships,
Do they serve popcorn with their quips?
While we fumble with earthly woes,
They're cracking jokes from distant shows.

So let's shout our dreams to the sky,
And maybe one day we'll learn to fly.
For in the chase, the fun is found,
In whispers of stars, our laughter resounds!

Secrets Beneath the Surface

Underneath the waves, fish whisper low,
Do they know things that we don't sow?
With bubbles rising, secrets unfurl,
Splashing dreams in a watery whirl.

The octopus giggles, flipping through books,
Comments on life with quirky looks.
"Why swim straight when you can twirl?"
He laughs as he makes the ocean swirl.

Coral reefs hiding treasures bright,
Even the seaweed dances at night.
But what of our dreams? Changeless, it seems,
They sink below in restless streams.

Let's dive deep, but take a float,
For wisdom swims with a silly coat.
In secrets held, let's find our jest,
The aquatic giggles, surely the best!

Tides of Purpose

Waves crash in with a quirky splash,
Declarations loud, but thoughts like ash.
What is it that we truly seek?
A beach ball dance or a game of peek?

Seagulls laugh, mistake us for fries,
While we ponder over endless skies.
If life's a puzzle, what's the key?
Is it buried in sand? Maybe a genie!

Kites soaring high, our spirits too,
On the winds of laughter, we break through.
Chasing purpose like a rolling stone,
But joy's the treasure we call our own.

So let the tides take us where they please,
Worry not, we'll dance in the breeze.
For with each wave, let giggles surge,
In the journey, let our spirits merge!

Kites Against the Wind

Flying high, we chase the breeze,
Tangled strings, oh what a tease.
The sky's a laugh, so bright and blue,
Who knew that kites could feel askew?

Laughter sails with every glide,
In the air, our dreams collide.
Why worry about the ground below?
We're just here to steal the show!

Clouds are friends, they float and play,
As we dance in our own way.
Reality's just paper thin,
Let's soar where whimsy does begin!

Kites may tangle in a tree,
But that's where all the fun will be.
A leap, a laugh, we're flying high,
With silly thoughts, we touch the sky!

Portraits of Uncertainty

Brush in hand, I sketch my fate,
Each line wobbles, it won't wait.
A canvas full of curious shapes,
Wondering if they'll escape.

Faces grin, then change their tune,
Silly rabbits under the moon.
Who's the artist, who's the fool?
In a world that's lost its cool!

Colors clash and laughter spills,
The gallery gives us all the thrills.
Uncertainty's the muse I seek,
With every stroke, I find the peak!

So here's to blunders, cheers in tow,
For every 'oops' that helps us grow.
Portraits of joy, absurd and bright,
In the art of life, we find our light!

Threads of Infinity

Spinning yarns of tales untold,
Each thread a giggle, bright and bold.
Weaves of laughter, knots of cheer,
Twisting stories year by year.

A tapestry of silly dreams,
Where nothing's ever what it seems.
Infinity's just a tangled strand,
Hold on tight, we'll make a band!

Life's a quilt with patches wild,
The fabric's frayed, but oh so styled.
We stitch together laughs and sighs,
In this odd patchwork, joy complies!

So let's embrace the random thread,
In the chaos, laughter's spread.
With each new twist, we'd never part,
These threads of whimsy, purest art!

The Dance of Whimsy

Pick up your feet, let's start the reel,
With every turn, we spin and squeal.
The floor's a stage, the lights are bright,
We'll dance our worries into the night.

Step to the left, now jump and glide,
Life's a carnival, come take a ride!
Clumsy steps, but hearts so free,
It's just a party, you'll see!

Frolic and twirl, embrace the fun,
Under the moon, let's run, run, run!
With every laugh, we shake the ground,
In our frolic, joy is found.

So when in doubt, let joy unfold,
In this whimsical dance, we break the mold.
Laughter's the beat, let's keep the score,
In the dance of life, we'll always soar!

The Art of Becoming

In a world of hats, I try them on,
Today I'm a chef, tomorrow a con!
With shoes on the wrong feet, I skip and dance,
Life's a game of chance, not a solemn prance.

I'll juggle my dreams, and drop a few,
Laughing at failures, oh yes, quite a view!
Each misstep a masterpiece, a work of art,
Unraveling life from the very start.

So hand me a canvas, or maybe a broom,
I'll paint my chaos, let creativity bloom!
Just remember, dear friend, don't take it too hard,
Life's meant to be funny, a wild zoo yard!

And when all is said, and I draw my last breath,
I'll say I had fun, not fearing the death!
With chuckles and giggles, in my final act,
A jest on my lips, that's a true life fact.

Transience and Legacy

A paper boat floats on a puddle so deep,
I wave it goodbye, then I trip and I leap.
It spins in the ripples, a fleeting delight,
Just like all our worries, they vanish from sight.

We build our grand towers, of sand and of dreams,
But watch them dissolve in the sun's golden beams.
Yet in every crash, every tumble and fall,
We're legends of laughter, oh yes, that's us all!

So cherish the moments, the slips and the slides,
For life's like a carnival, chaos abides.
In poorly drawn stencils, our stories are told,
In every blunder, we find hidden gold.

At the end of the show, when the laughter has ceased,
We'll leave behind giggles, our funniest feast.
For if I can witness your quirkiest grin,
Then maybe, just maybe, we both truly win!

Carvings in Time

They say time is a river, flowing away,
With stones like my dreams, they roll and they sway.
I chisel this moment, a block's full of cheer,
A goofy grin frozen, and let out a tear.

I carve out a memory, a noodle on plate,
With visions of dancing, I giggle at fate.
A tree's twisted branches are stories that bend,
Creating a jungle where myths never end.

The clocks tick in rhythm, a waltz of the past,
Yet I notice the daisies, their colors so vast.
Time is a jester, a playful old soul,
And each tick of laughter is a step toward whole.

So here's to the carvings, both messy and grand,
To the slips in our steps, and the joy in the sand.
With every mistake, a tale to unfurl,
A funny existence in this whimsical swirl.

Stories of Starlight

Under the cosmos, I spin and I twirl,
With stories of starlight, my dreams gently swirl.
I catch falling stars, all wearing odd hats,
They giggle and shimmer, like comical chats.

I paint them with giggles, bright yellow and blue,
Each twinkle a secret, a joke or two.
They toss me their wishes, and I laugh out loud,
Sharing my tales with the adventurous crowd.

A comet zooms by, wearing socks on its tail,
While planets debate if it's worth it to sail.
The universe hums with a silly old tune,
As I dance with the night, and juggle the moon.

So here's to the stories, the laughs in the night,
To the chuckles we share in the soft silver light.
When we look to the sky, and find joy in the fright,
We're all little whimsies, in the grand starry night.

The Gardener's Secrets of Growth

In the garden where weeds play,
The carrots giggle and sway.
Tomatoes whisper in the sun,
Sharing secrets of their fun.

Chasing bugs with silly dances,
While giving plants their chances.
Weed removal: a funny act,
Like searching for a socks' lost pact.

Rainclouds grumble, but who cares?
They join in games, splitting their hairs.
Sprouts peek out with a sneaky grin,
In this jungle, we'll always win!

So, grab a trowel, take a swing,
Join our garden's crazy fling.
With laughter we will till the soil,
Growing joy through every toil.

Ephemeral Moments

Bubbles float on the summer breeze,
Reflecting wonders, oh so sweet!
They burst with laughter, then they're gone,
Like fleeting thoughts at break of dawn.

Jumping puddles, splashing high,
Raincoats worn like superstars in the sky.
Each drop a giggle, a dance, a cheer,
Moments cherished, year to year.

A wink from time as it drifts away,
Reminding us to laugh, to play.
So catch the whimsy, hold it tight,
For in a flash, it takes to flight.

Life's a game of hopscotch bliss,
Don't miss a leap, or a joyful kiss.
In the blink of an eye, it's all a show,
So smile wide, let the goodness flow!

Eternal Echoes

Whispers travel through the trees,
Carried gently, like a breeze.
They chuckle tales of forgotten days,
Replaying laughter in strange ways.

Footsteps echo on sunlit trails,
Where dreams are woven with fairy tales.
Ghosts of giggles linger on,
Dancing silhouettes from dusk till dawn.

In the park where laughter swells,
Every heart has stories to tell.
Even silence hums a tune,
Under the watch of the playful moon.

So listen close and bend your ear,
For echoes of joy are always near.
They skip and bounce, they run and play,
Turning mundane into a cabaret!

The Voice Behind Closed Eyes

In dreams we giggle, jump, and sing,
Imagination takes its wing.
A talking cat, a dancing shoe,
Every night, it's something new.

Behind closed eyes, the world's a show,
Wacky hairstyles, a cosmos glow.
Bananas hanging from the moon,
It's a silly, zany cartoon!

Hats made of yarn, and socks that fly,
Tickle fights with clouds in the sky.
The sandman knows our truest laughs,
Every dream, we're virtual puffs!

So, close your eyes and take the leap,
To worlds where shenanigans never sleep.
In the land of snooze, let's fondly roam,
Discovering fun far away from home!

Stories Written in Invisible Ink

Once upon a time, tales went awry,
Written with a wink and a sly sigh.
Invisible ink on a napkin bright,
Waiting for laughter to spark delight.

Bouncing off walls, these stories hide,
In the laughter of friends, they bide.
A giggle here, a chuckle there,
Each whispers of joy in the air.

Hidden tales, oh what a treat,
Like sneaky snacks that can't be beat.
Follow your heart, find what is real,
In the silly things, we all can heal.

So scribble your dreams and make them fly,
Transform the mundane, let your heart sigh.
For in this world, we've got the link,
To all our stories in invisible ink!

Chronicles of the Unseen

In a cupboard, dust bunnies play,
Whispers of secrets, they giggle all day.
They dream of the world outside their door,
While searching for crumbs, they find so much more.

A missing sock gives a rabbit a rise,
Claiming it's proof of a sock fashion prize.
They host a parade, each one dressed so bright,
In mismatched old garments, they dance through the night.

The cat, a judge, with a skeptical glare,
Evaluates style with an elegant air.
But who needs approval when fun's in the mix?
All join in the revels with wild, crazy tricks.

So next time you ponder what lives in the dark,
Remember the laughter, the fun, and the spark.
Life's more than a lesson, it's joyful surprise,
With bunnies and socks and cats donning ties.

Lanterns in the Dark

Moonlight spills over the laughter we share,
As fireflies waltz with a flicker of flair.
We chase down the shadows, we trip and we fall,
While listening closely to night's playful call.

A wise old owl chimes in with a wink,
Offering riddles that make us all think.
"Why did the chicken cross over the road?"
We're giggling too hard—what a riddle bestowed!

The stars join the fun, twinkling with glee,
Competing for laughter, not just to be free.
In the dark, we find lanterns to light our way,
With each silly venture, brightening the play.

So let's gather round and embrace the unknown,
For laughter's the lantern we've brightly outgrown.
In this cosmic joke, we laugh and we sway,
Life's just a punchline, let's shout "hooray!"

Memories in Mosaic

Jigsaw puzzles of thought, scattered and bright,
Each piece tells a story, a laugh, or a fright.
I found one of pizza, but double the cheese,
A memory placed like a wonky trapeze.

A broken alarm clock, it sleeps through the day,
Reminds me of moments we wished far away.
"Just five more minutes," we'd endlessly plead,
Yet time ticked away like an ungrateful seed.

Then came the old video, blurry with age,
Of dancing like goofs on a comical stage.
We cringed and we giggled at outfits so bold,
As history danced, its story retold.

So cherish these moments, both silly and grand,
They make up the mosaic that's perfectly planned.
In laughter and chaos, our tales intertwine,
Painting life's canvas, each memory a line.

Questions at Dusk

As twilight descends, questions start to bloom,
"Is a hotdog a sandwich?!" it fills up the room.
The crickets chime in with their chirps and their clicks,
While pondering mysteries that give us the kicks.

"Why does a lemon go sour in the sun?"
"Can turtles race, or are they just fun?"
We ponder the colors of clouds in the sky,
And giggle at whimsy as day waves goodbye.

The stars start to emerge with a glittery grin,
While debating if penguins should ever wear skin.
"Can fish really feel all that wetness they swim?"
Life's questions are funny; it's hard not to brim!

So let's raise a glass to the charm of the night,
For each silly question, there's laughter in sight.
In the dance of the dusk, let our wonders unroll,
For the quirks of the cosmos bring joy to the soul.

www.ingramcontent.com/pod-product-compliance
Ingram Content Group UK Ltd.
Pitfield, Milton Keynes, MK11 3LW, UK
UKHW021652160125
4146UKWH00033B/712